# WATER'S WAY

# WATER'S WAY

By Lisa Westberg Peters

Illustrated by Ted Rand

Arcade Publishing / New York

LITTLE, BROWN AND COMPANY

Water has a way of changing. It can rise from the sea or fall from the clouds. It can drift in a fog or lie still on a winter pond.

Every day, water is changing, all across the land and sea and sky, and changing inside Tony's house, too.

It was early winter. Outside, a breeze blew in to the hills and the smell of the sea filled the morning air.

Inside, Tony kept an eye on the sky and a hand on his brand new sled. He was hoping for snow. Behind him, steam rose from a pot on the stove and the smell of soup filled the room.

When the moist breeze from the sea met the hills, it rose and cooled off.
Clouds formed in the sky.

When the steam from the soup pot hit the cool kitchen window, it covered the glass with a foggy curtain.

Outside, a few raindrops splashed on the ground. The air wasn't cold enough for snow. Soon houses and hillsides shimmered behind the sheets of rain.

Inside, Tony wrote his name on the fogged window and peeked through.
Drips streaked down the glass from each letter.

Some of the rain collected into puddles. Some of it soaked into the ground, and tree roots sucked it from the soil. Some of it seeped into the earth where it would creep through the rocks.

A tiny puddle formed on Tony's windowsill. Tony poked at it. There'd be no sledding today.

In the warmth of the afternoon sun, roofs dried out. Puddles shrank. Evergreens lost their glisten.

In the kitchen, the fog on the glass and the puddle on the windowsill disappeared.

By evening, a nearby creek grew wide and full from the day's rain. It surged
downhill, down to the sea.

After supper, Tony climbed the stairs for his bath. He turned on the tap full blast and a steamy torrent filled the tub.

When the creek reached the sea, salty waves washed in and out, around and around, until the creek blended into the sea.

When Tony stepped in for his bath, he added a few drops of green soap. He sailed his boats in and out, around and around his bathtub ocean, until the green streams faded and blurred.

The wind stirred up the surf and a bit of the sea escaped into the sky. It was invisible, but the smell of the sea filled the air.

Tony whipped up bubbles in his ocean and the smell of soap filled the room.

As the breeze from the sea met cooler air over the land, tiny drops formed around specks of dust. Each drop was too small to see, but together they made clouds.

As Tony headed for bed, he found another window clouded, this time from his bath.

That night, the air turned cold, cold enough for the tiny drops in the clouds to freeze into ice crystals. They grew larger and heavier.

All night, Tony dreamed of sledding. He stayed warm and cozy beneath a mound of blankets. But the fog on the bathroom window froze into a frosty curtain.

By dawn, the clouds were thick with ice crystals. The larger ones, too heavy to float, began to fall.

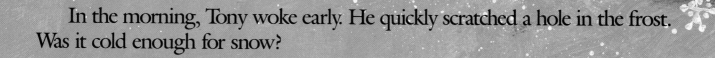

In the morning, Tony woke early. He quickly scratched a hole in the frost. Was it cold enough for snow?

Houses and hillsides vanished behind a wild flurry of snowflakes. The snow settled on the rooftops and the evergreens. It covered the new layer of ice on the puddles.

A snowflake landed on Tony's face. He wished it would last forever, but it soon melted in his smile because . . .

water has a way of changing.

To my daughter-in-law: Deb Henry Rand—T.R.

ACKNOWLEDGMENTS

The author would like to thank Gregory J. Spoden of the Minnesota
State Climatology Office, Professor E. Calvin Alexander, Jr., of the
Department of Geology and Geophysics at the University of Minnesota,
and Julie Amper for their help with this book.

First Edition

Library of Congress Cataloging-in-Publication Data

Peters, Lisa Westberg.
    Water's way / by Lisa Westberg Peters ; illustrated by Ted Rand.—1st ed.
    p.    cm.
Summary: Introduces the different forms that water can have, from clouds to
steam to fog.
ISBN 1-55970-062-9
1. Water—Juvenile literature.  [1. Water.]  I. Rand, Ted, ill.  II. Title.
GB662.3.P48  1991
551.46—dc20  90-55648                                                    90-55648

Published in the United States
by Arcade Publishing, Inc., New York, a Little, Brown company

*Published simultaneously in Canada*
*by Little, Brown & Company (Canada) Limited*

Printed in the United States of America
Designed by Marc Cheshire
WOR

1 3 5 7 9 10 8 6 4 2